Hawaii Blossoms

Text and Color Photography

by

Dorothy and Bob Hargreaves

First Printing 1958
Copyright in Japan / Dorothy and Bob Hargreaves

Published by
HARGREAVES COMPANY
P.O. BOX 895 · KAILUA, HAWAII 96734

Price $2.00 in U.S. funds, postpaid anywhere in the world
from the publisher. Also available at bookstores.

AIR PLANT

Bryophyllum pinnatum (Lam) KURZ

The Hawaiians call this Oliwa-Ku-Kahakai—beach oleander because the first one was reportedly seen near the beach.

It is a wild succulent plant that grows quite numerously on the lower slopes of Mt. Tantalus and elsewhere in the Hawaiian foothills. The blooms are a funny little shaped pinkish-green balloon-like cylinder. They grow on a tall spike from the center of the plant. The leaves, true to their name, grow on air. One can pin a leaf on a curtain and soon the humid air of the Islands produces tiny roots from each little groove of the scalloped shiny-thick leaf. An entirely separate plant will then soon develop. Blooms usually in spring. Will grow indoors on the mainland.

GOLD TREE
(See page 43)

YELLOW ALLAMANDA

Allamanda cathartica
var. *hendersonii* (Bull) RAFFILL

These are called Lani-alii—meaning Heavenly Chief
—by the Hawaiians. They are large, velvety, golden-
yellow flowers growing on sprawling vines or shrubs.
The tube spreads into five thick lobes with two or
three buds opening at a time. They are pointed,
brownish in color and look as if they had been var-
nished. The leaves are smooth, thick and pointed.
Periwinkle family from Brazil. It is used as a cathartic.

AMARYLLIS—
Amaryllidaceae

BARBADOS LILY

Hippeastrum equestre

This lily of many colors is from a bulb from which it rises one to two feet high. It has lovely showy flower trumpets. The one pictured was growing wild on Kauai (note weeds in background). Blooms in the spring. Grows outdoors on the mainland in the summer.

SPIDER LILY

Hymenocallis littoralis (Jacq.) SALISB.

This was a favorite of Queen Emma. It blooms constantly and is seen in many places on the islands. It is a liliaceous plant with six thin spidery petals and six stamens. The botany of these lilies has been much confused in Hawaii. The leaves are two to six feet long and grow in a large clump. The flowers are very fragrant. Came from tropical America where they are used medicinally.

3

ANTHURIUM, Flamingo Flower

Anthurium andraeanum LINDEN

This is a most popular Hawaiian exotic flower because it will last as long as three weeks if cut in its prime. It is a beautiful waxen member of the Arum family (Calla Lily is also a member of this family). It ranges in color from pure white, pink-red, deep red, orange, red and green and many others. The flower is really a heart-shaped bract called the spathe. It is thick and waxen and looks artificial. From this spathe rises the spadix, white, pinkish, or yellow. The true flowers are on this spadix and are hardly noticeable. The leaves too are large, lovely, heart-shaped and nicely veined. The larger the leaves, the larger the flowers. It is a native of tropical America. Some plants are valued at $100 or more apiece. Can be grown in Hapu as a houseplant on the mainland.

APE

Alocasia macrorrhiza SCHOTT

Pronounced "Ah-pay." Very large, heart-shaped
leaves from four to five feet high shelter strange
flowers up to a foot long. They are related to the
Taro. Have rather an unpleasant odor. They come
from Asia and usually bloom in the spring. Their
milky juice is said to relieve pain from nettle
stings. Found on grounds of Royal Hawaiian Hotel and Mormon Temple.

BEAUMONTIA VINE

Beaumontia jerdoniana WIGHT

Big white blooms with a pinkish-brown cast to the outside petals mark this delicately fragranted vine from India as one to be favored in the Islands. A member of the Periwinkle family, the flower is about six inches across. It has five lobes. The centers are a pale green. Five white stamens which join at their tips arise from within. The flowers are used in wedding bouquets. The leaves are large, smooth, deeply veined and pointed. Bloom winter and spring. There is a vine at Mrs. Beaumont's gardens, Cooper Road at Hillside.

BIRD OF PARADISE

Strelitzia reginae BANKS

The exotic coloring and looks of this flower is undoubtedly known to all. The tall stalks look like the neck of a bird topped by a lovely head with a long beak and crest. This beak is a pointed sheath, greyish-blue in color. The crest of the bird is made up of flowers lifting out of this sheath. Usually about six to a sheath. One pushes out every day or so. Thus the cluster becomes larger and more colorful as it becomes older. Flower has three pointed petals, brilliant orange with blue staminodiums shaped like arrowheads. The flower stalks grow slightly above the clump of stiff paddle-shaped leaves which are about three or four feet long with a reddish vein down the center. They are a relative of the banana and a native of South Africa. Bloom intermittently.

WHITE BIRD OF PARADISE

Strelitzia nicolai THUNBERG

Curious flowers that grow on a small tree that looks like a palm. They have banana-like leaves. Look much like their relative, the Orange and Blue Bird. The sheath is purplish-blue-grey color, and is frequently smeared with a gummy substance as pictured. Hawaiian Village, Breakers, etc.

7

BOUGAINVILLEA
**Is named from a French navigator
Louis A. de Bougainville.**

CRIMSON LAKE BOUGAINVILLEA

Bougainvillea glabra, var *Sanderiana choisy*

These are long, colorful sprays of bright crimson flowers which are grown
on the close cousin of the purple species (*B. spectabilis*) pictured right.
The leaves are small and triangular with wavy margins. The stems have
thorns. They bloom in winter, spring, and early summer. Can be seen
on Punahou campus, St. Louis campus, etc.; other colors also. Native
of Brazil.

NIGHTBLOOMING CEREUS

Hylocereus undatus (Haw.) BRITT and ROSE

Hawaiians call this Panini-o-Kapunahou. It is a well known flower of the Islands, yet, strangely enough, it is a Mexican Cactus brought from Acapulco in the early days by a seaman. He presented it to a missionary teacher who planted it on the Punahou campus. It is still there.

It opens huge buds about eight in the evening between June and October. A climber with fleshy, three-sided stems, scalloped and spiny, it pushes up walls, banks, trees and so forth for lengths up to sixty feet. Buds appear as tiny bright colored cones, increasing until they are almost a foot long, egg-shaped and enclosed in greenish yellow sepals. One can watch these sepals and petals unfold to a beautiful bloom filled with many pale yellow stamens. The style is among these stamens like an individual flower (see picture). The Cereus only remains open until the sun and heat of the day wilts it. Then it droops and closes — a lovely flower presented to the world for a fleeting glimpse. (Also *Selenicereus grandiflorus* [L.] nightblooming Rope Cactus, Snake Cactus.)

CHENILLE PLANT

Acalypha hispida Burmann

This strange looking tropical shrub from the East Indies where it is used medicinally, has long velvety tails of dark red up to eighteen inches long which resemble chenille for which they are named. These tails are made up of staminate flowers with no petals. They have dark green veined rather pointed leaves. May be found on the Royal Hawaiian Hotel grounds and in Foster Gardens Greenhouse.

(Note the Beefsteak Hedge—*Acalypha wilkesiana* J. Mueller-Aargau. Background left.)

CROWN FLOWER or Giant Indian Milkweed

Calotropis gigantea LINNAEUS AITON

The Hawaiians call this common lei flower "Pua Kalaunu." They use it in several ways for leis. The center crown alone can be used. The whole flower can be used, or it can be made into a Mauna Loa type lei by breaking the center crown in two. The leaves are light grey-green, round and deeply veined. The butterflies love the milky juices. These juices are toxic to many people. The bush belongs to the milkweed family from India. It was popular with Queen Liliuokalani as it resembled a crown. White and lavender varieties.

CUP OF GOLD, Golden Cup

Solandra nitida Zucc.
(Commonly misdetermined as *S. guttata* Don)

A spectacular flower with blossoms up to nine inches long. Quite large, they bloom for four days, changing in color from light cream when in bud, to a golden banana color when in full bloom, to an orangish-apricot before it dies (smells a little like ripe apricots, too).

The huge, waxy buds unfold almost before your eyes. It is a member of the potato family. A native of Mexico and Tropical America. The Spanish call it "Copa de Oro." It can be a sixty-foot jungle climber. Blooms in winter and spring on way to Punchbowl, Tantalus, etc.

RED GINGER, Ostrich Plume Ginger

Alpinia purpurata (Vieillard) SCHUMANN

The long, pretty red bracts of these showy flowers look like the bloom, but the true flower is a small whitish bloom which appears from behind these bracts (see picture). The leaves come out gracefully alternate along the stem. It is a good flower for flower arrangements. Native of Malaya. Blooms most of the year.

TORCH GINGER

Phaeomeria magnifica (Roscoe) SCHUMANN

The fifteen-foot bamboo-like stalks with large, bright green leaf blades, not unlike a small forest, practically conceal the spectacular torch bloom that springs up like an independent plant three to six feet tall besides the leaf stalks. These are one of the showy heads of the world! The cone is made up of many bracts shaped like a torch. Looks unreal in its waxen-like glory. Native of the Netherlands East Indies. Can be seen in Foster Gardens in spring.

13

YELLOW GINGER

Zingiber zerumbet L. SMITH

The Hawaiians call these lovely wild ginger "Awapuhi-Kuahiwi, Opuhi." The delicately fragrant light yellow blossom rises at the end of a narrow tube composed of olive colored bracts. One blossom emerges from behind each bract. They consist of three petals and three sepals. The leaves are luxuriant big green alternates similar to the Red Ginger. The flowers are used for leis. Native of India. Blooms summer and fall.

SHELL GINGER

Alpinia nutans (Andres) ROSCOE

The shell-like flowers which spill out of the top of the twelve-foot stalk have an almost porcelain texture. They are white tipped in delicate pink. The flowers push out one at a time. They are light yellow with fine red lines. On the stalk, the alternate leaves are big blades five inches wide and up to two feet long. Prolific bloomers. Native of tropical East Asia.

14

HELICONIA
Name Heliconia comes from Mt. Helicon in Greece

Heliconia elongata

This unreal looking exotic has a pinkish sheath edged with yellow and green. These large bracts make spectacular and long lasting flower arrangements.

15

HELICONIA
HANGING HELICONIA
Heliconia collinsiana GRIGGS

These bracts are similar to the Lobster Claw (see picture on next page). They, too, have bright red keels, but they jut out of the stem and instead of going up straight as the Lobster Claw they hang gracefully toward the ground. They have striking bright yellow flowers inside this keel.

Smaller Heliconia often used in yard plantings. (See picture at left.)

HELICONIA — LOBSTER CLAW

Heliconia sp. 1 also *Heliconia humilis* JACQUIN

This heliconia grows in a clump of tall, paddle-shaped leaves (Banana family). The real flowers are inconspicuous inside the sheaths that are so colorful. They are a native of Tropical America. The bracts are bright red and suggest the red of boiled lobster claws—excellent for flower arranging.

HIBISCUS
Malvaceae (80 genera and 1000 species)
Natives call this the "Kokio Aloalo."

In 1923 it was so decided by joint resolution of the legislature that this would be the floral emblem of Hawaii. It is the outstanding flower of the South Seas.

You see Hibiscus most anywhere you look or go in Hawaii. There are all sizes, shapes and colors. The women wear them tucked in their hair. Samoan men wear them behind their ears when they dance. You see them laying on the tables, desks, counters, strewn down lengths of luau tables, arranged in beautiful displays (Royal Hawaiian Hotel's Hibiscus Tree), in banks, Temples and hotels. They are unique as no other flower as they possess the trait of not wilting for a day after picking. Whether on the shrub, or laid out for all to behold, they remain fresh and beautiful until nightfall when they quietly close and fade—a lovely gift to the world for the brief span of a day.

CORAL HIBISCUS
Hibiscus schizopetalus HOOKER

This is the parent of many Island hybrids. It is a dainty little coral colored Hibiscus with a slender and graceful curving stem. The petals are frilled and lacy.

HYBRID HIBISCUS

As crossing is easy, there are many, many species of Hybrid Hibiscus. The pollen of one flower dabbled on the pistil of another, after its pollen is removed, produces seeds in a month and will blossom in a year.

Hibiscus bloom most of the year. They may be seen in the Foster Gardens, many hotel grounds—Hawaiian Village, Royal Hawaiian, Halekulani, etc.

They have five petals, five stigmas, five lobes to calyx (like the Hollyhock, a relative). They usually grow upright, but when they gracefully curve they are related to the Coral Hibiscus (see left page).

Throughout the world the Hibiscus furnishes beauty, food (Okra), medicine, perfume, dye, etc.

HAU TREE
Hibiscus tiliaceus LINNAEUS

This is pronounced — "how." It is a true Hibiscus. It is used for training into arbors as the branches interlock and form a roof overhead. There is one called the "Hau Lanai" at the Halekulani Hotel with a gnarled and twisted central trunk several feet thick. The flowers of the Hau are bright yellow as pictured with a dark throat at the center. As they grow older during the day, they turn to apricot color, and as they get ready to drop at nightfall, they turn a deep red.

TURK'S CAP
Malvaviscus arboreus CAVANILLES

This is a funny little flower like a closed red Hibiscus. It looks like the red Shriner's or Turk's Fez.

IXORA

Ixora macrothyrsa Teijsmann
and Binnendijk

This is a member of the Coffee
family from Malaya. It blooms
in March and April. The big,
bright, round 'snowball' heads of
scarlet blossoms are very showy.
They grow up to fifteen feet high.
The small individual flowers have
four petals and these grouped to-
gether make a big round ball up
to six inches across.

There are smaller bushes, too, with pale reddish-orange blossoms—see
inset. Both shrubs have large glossy foliage.

JADE VINE

Strongylodon macrobotrys A. GREY

This Legume of the pea subfamily is from the Philippines. It may be seen in full array at the Foster Gardens in the spring. The vine hangs down among its leaves to several feet. The flower of this unusual Jade colored vine is like an individual cornicopia two inches long. They are not easily pollinated because the long pea-shaped keels do not open naturally and let the bees in at the pollen. They are now being used as leis which are long lasting and unusual.

MEXICAN CREEPER, Mountain Rose, Chain of Love

Antigonon leptopus HOOKER and ARNOTT

Found along the banks, in hedges, and clambering beside the road is this lacy, bright, pink flower. It is a native of Latin America (Mexico) where it is called Cadena del Amor— Chain of Love.

The flowers suggest strings of small pink hearts. They have no petals. The flowers are calyx with five petal-like sepals. Leaves, too, are heart-shaped with wavy margins. They belong to the buckwheat family. Bloom in early spring. Also white and light pink color.

OLEANDER

Nerium oleander LINNAEUS

Hawaiians call this Oliwa, Oleana, or Oliana. It is of the Periwinkle family, and it is from Asia Minor. Shrubs grow up to twenty feet tall, but the average is about eight to ten feet. The leaves are slender, pointed and a dull green. The branches are tipped with clusters of flowers of all colors, some single with five petals, others double. The colors range from white through cream, pink, rose, red, etc. The shrub is poisonous. Even insects do not bother it. Food cooked on the wood can even poison. Blooms continuously.

ORANGE TRUMPET VINE, Flame Flower, Firecracker Vine

Pyrostegia ignea (Vell) PRESL. or *Bignonia venusta* KER.

Hawaiians call this Huapala, meaning sweetheart. From January through April, this blazing vine is a most spectacular sight to behold. The flowers are long, slender tubes with four or five lobes which curl gently back. The leaves are bright green, pointed and glossy. It is a native of Brazil. (*see cover picture*)

ORCHIDS—some 700 species

A separate book could be written about orchids. The greenhouse at Foster Gardens houses an excellent collection of orchids. Also there are many nurseries and private homes that grow orchids similar to the Vanda Hybrid pictured above.

WILD, or Philippine Orchid

Spathoglottis plicata BLUME

Grows wild on the trails (Sacred Falls near Punaluu, near the Pali). Has graceful, tapering leaves, many ridged, from which rise the flowering stalks of heads of small flowers. Usually these are lavender and purple, but there are some pink, white, and yellow ones. They bloom in the spring. There are some wild orchids outside the greenhouse at Foster Gardens.

PAGODA FLOWER

Clerodendron squamatum VAHL.

Hawaiians call this Lau 'awa. A native of Java. These bright red flowers bloom in large, rather loose, upright heads. The individual flowers are five narrow lobes which turn back against the tube. The stamens and pistil curve beyond this flower in small red tufts. The leaves are large, heart-shaped, thick and velvety with deep veins. The stems are downy. Shrub grows about ten feet tall.

PRICKLY PEAR

Opuntia megacantha SALM-DYCH
(formerly known as *O tuna* [L] MILLER)

The Hawaiians call this Panini (very unfriendly), Nini, pa-wall. They make a fermented drink from the fruit and also eat it raw.

A cactus typical of the Mexican ones grows in profusion on the arid slopes of Hawaii.

It was introduced in about 1800. It grows to a height of fifteen feet. Has yellow or orange flowers up to three inches in diameter from which develop pear shaped fruit about three inches long.

PIKAKE, Arabian Jasmine

(Queen Emma's flower) *Jasminum sambac*

Little white, very sweet smelling flowers with nine or ten petals make into a very special strand of leis. It looks like a tiny rose when in full bloom, but only the buds are picked just before they open and strung into the lovely Pikake leis. Pikake is Hawaiian and means "Peacock" because the Princess Kaiulani was fond of the flower and peacocks, too. The leaves are small and shiny. The bush grows to about waist high. Belongs to the Olive family, from India. They are used commercially for perfume, too. There are Pikake Gardens at 4192 Huanui Street.

POINSETTIA

Euphorbia pulcherrima Willdenow

The flower that is the symbol of Christmas belongs to the Spurge family from Mexico. The Poinsettias that bloom so beautifully in Hawaii are usually double with huge shaggy heads of many red leaves. They bloom for a long period of time as hedges, shrubs and spectacular yard plantings. If untrimmed, they will grow to twelve feet or more, but they flower better if cut back once or twice a year. There is a lovely hedge around the Mormon Temple. They bloom by the length of time they receive daylight. Thus are called a "short day" bloomer, and so usually bloom in November and December when the days are shorter. Brilliant street lights have postponed blooming period. Also white and pink.

SHRIMP PLANT

Beloperone guttata BRANDEGEE

These rosy-brown bracts that are heart
shaped overlap each other on a curving
stem. This makes them suggest a scale
that looks like the curved tail of the
shrimp—thus the name. The true flowers
are white and tubular with purplish veins
on the lower lip of two lobes. Acanthus
family from Mexico. Gardens of Royal
Hawaiian Hotel.

WHITE SHRIMP PLANT,
Squirrels Tails

Justicia betonica

Green and white spikes of heart shaped
bracts with green veins. True flower is
lavender and white. ᐟ

32

SPATHIPHYLLUM

S. clevelandii (Hybrid of *S. kochii*)

A blossom like a small, white Anthurium only more fragile looking. The leaves grow about two feet high, are long, pointed and blade-like in very rich dark green. They are used for low-growing cover in shady tropical gardens. They do not last when cut, however. This is the common species grown around Honolulu, but it is not in botanical literature. It is a horticultural name. It is a member of the Arum family from tropical America. Blooms intermittently. Royal Hawaiian.

STEPHANOTIS

Stephanotis floribunda BRONGNIART

The Hawaiians call this Pua Male—Marriage flower. It is the familiar wedding bouquet flower. They are waxy, white, fragrant, trumpet-shaped flowers (look and smell a little like the individual flowers of the hyacinths). The flowers are about two inches long with five lobes. They hang in clusters of six or eight on the vine. Leis are often made of them. The leaves are thick and glossy. Belongs to the milkweed family from Madagascar. (Note the seed pod.)

WOODEN ROSE, Wood Rose

Ipomoea tuberosa LINNAEUS

(Sometimes called the Ceylon Morning-glory and Spanish Arbor Vine)

Known as Pilikai, Kowali, or Koali to the Hawaiians. The Wood Rose is well known to the tourist of Hawaii. It is a vine of strange and attractive appearance. Looks like a rose carved of wood and polished to a beautiful satiny-brown finish. Actually, it is the dried seed pod of a species of morning-glory. (See the yellow blooms in the picture.) The central bulb contains the seeds. This is surrounded by graceful dried petals (calyx). It is a perennial which grows from seed. The shoots spread rampantly during the summer months covering trees, buildings, fences and whole fields. Blooms in the spring. The yellow flowers fall and the calyx begins to develop enlarging into large, pointed, cream-colored buds. These dry and open and in a few days, the "Wood Rose" is stiff and beautiful. It takes three months from blossom to rose. Used for lasting dried arrangements. An excellent vine is located behind Trader Hall's on the Windward side of Oahu.

AFRICAN TULIP TREE

Spathodea campanulata BEAUVOIS

The fiery red flowers of this large tree grow in circular groups around closely crowded buds. These buds develop a few at a time thus insuring blooms the year around. They have five irregular, frilled lobes. The edges of the corolla are vivid yellow while the inside of the cup is yellow with red streaks. They grow out of spathe-like calyx deriving generic name *Spathodea*. The pods up to two feet long are boat-shaped. The leaves are large and compound. They are made up of three or four pairs, dark green in color, with leathery, heavy veining. Bignonia family native of tropical Africa. Examples in Manoa, on Kahala Avenue,Makiki, and an excellent avenue of trees is on University Avenue at Kaala. Very beautiful to behold.

ANGEL'S TRUMPET TREE

Datura candida (Pers) PASQUALE

The Hawaiians call this "Nana Honua" which means gazing earthward. When viewing the many trumpets "gazing earthward" one might feel that the tiny Menehunes must have placed these large big white trumpet-shaped flowers on the small tree (fifteen feet high) for a Christmas Tree. They are around ten inches long and have five thin segments each coming to a twisted point. They give off an exotic scent of musk. The leaves are large, greyish-green, thick and velvety. Lower Tantalus has some, also Kahala Avenue. Bloom intermittently. Flowers and leaves are poisonous to eat. The whole plant contains a strong narcotic. In Hawaii the plant is sometimes miscalled "belladonna."

BE-STILL, YELLOW OLEANDER

Thevetia peruviana (Pers.) K. SCHUM

A small tree, 20-foot maximum, with a scattering of trumpet-shaped yellow flowers. The leaves are fine, narrow and light green. They never seem to hold still, always shimmering in the wind, thus the name. They bloom the year around. It is a member of the Periwinkle family, not an Oleander. Native of tropical America. Noho Malie-Hawaiian.

BOMBAX

Bombax ellipticum HUMBOLDT, BONPLAND and KUNTH

Breathtaking pink plumes spring out from a bare tree like Ostrich Plumes. The bud, growing upright, is like a stubby cigar rising from the calyx. It splits into five parts, peels back like one peels a banana and curls. The lovely pink pompons with huge pink stamens five inches long jut out. From Mexico this unusual tree blooms March and and April on Queens Hospital grounds and Foster Gardens.

BOTTLEBRUSH TREE

Callistemon lanceolatus DE CANDOLLE

Long, cylindrical spikes of bright red flowers like the brushes used to clean bottles. This effect is created by small tufts of red stamens. The foliage is narrow, pointed and fine. It belongs to the Myrtle family from Australia. Specimens may be seen on University of Hawaii campus near Dean Hall. Spring.

BROWNEA

Brownea macrophylla LEUMINOSAE
(sometimes called Rouge Puff)

This spectacular flower pops out
of the limb of the tree like a big,
red pin cushion almost a foot
across. It is a small evergreen
tropical American tree which produces flowers directly on the trunk
in the spring. It has twelve pairs of
long narrow leathery leaflets.
Foster Gardens, Spring.

41

CANNONBALL TREE

Couroupita guianensis AUBLET

Huge trees with heavy bark produce these unusual flowers. The Cannonball limbs push right out of this heavy bark. The blooms are about five inches across. In some ways they look like the wood rose. They are a rosy-beige color and have a very sweet odor. Inside the six petals the staminal column has little yellow heads. The center is hook-shaped, the staminal end is fringed with stamens. The blossoms are followed by heavy, hard-shelled cannonball-like fruits six to eight inches across; have unpleasant odor. It is of the Brazil-nut family from Guiana. It is a deciduous tree that blossoms most of the time although they are most plentiful in the autumn. Foster Gardens.

GOLD TREE, SUNSHINE TREE, Primavera

Tabebuia donnell-smithii Rose syn. *Cybistax donnell-smithii* Rose

Probably one of the most spectacular floral events in Hawaii is the bloom-ing of the Gold Tree. This member of the Bignonia family from tropical America against the bright blue of the Hawaiian sky looks of pure gold. It brightens the day as sunshine. It is said that the flower blooms on the tips of the tree "like a touch of Midas." It is an irregular tube with five lobes having irregular margins. The leaves appear after the flowers fall. They are a compound form of opposite leaflets. The light grey trunk is smooth and the branches lift high in the sky. The time of the blooming of the Gold Tree is quite uncertain. Some spring into bloom in midwinter others choose spring. The original species was in Foster Gardens, planted by Dr. William Hillebrand, but has now been cut down. There is another tree on School Street also. There are some small trees in front of the DPW Build-ing across from Queens Hospital.

JACARANDA

Jacaranda acutifolia Humb. and Bonpl. syn *J. ovalifolia* R. Brown

One sees so many bright, warm colors in the Islands, that the cool blue of the Jacaranda is rather startling. These grow to large trees with light grey bark covered with foliage like a fern. The leaves are bipinnate and fall in late winter and early spring. The tree is then bare. The flowers appear about March in large, loose clusters at the ends of the branches. They are shaped like little blue bells. They have two lips, one with two, lobes, the other with three. They are a soft lavender-blue. Bignonia from Brazil. Found on Punahou campus, Makiki Heights Road, Manoa Road and East Manoa junction.

LEHUA HAOLE

Calliandra inaequilatera RUSBY

This small tree or shrub resembles the native Ohia (Ohia Lehua-*Metrosideros polymorpha* Gaudichaud) which grows on the cool high levels especially on the Island of Hawaii. Flower of Hawaii. It is a larger flower, however, and thrives at lower levels. The fluffy red pompons from which leis are made are very fragile in appearance. Look like little powder puffs. The leis are feathery and hold up quite well. Blooms in winter and early spring. Halekulani grounds, Foster Gardens. (Ohia Lehua, see page 48 "Tropical Trees of Hawaii" —*Hargreaves*.)

MONKEYPOD TREE, Rain Tree

Samanea saman (Jacq.) MERR.

The 'Ohai to Hawaiians; the Rain Tree to South Americans because legend has it that it "rains from the branches the juice of the cicadas."

This is one of the most symmetrical trees in the world, the wood of which is used to make the beautifully carved bowls and trays so typical of Hawaii. It has tiny pink tufts of stamens which pop up all over the semi-circular tree mostly in May and June. The leaves are tiny, fern-like leaflets compound four to eight pairs of pinnal leaves, much like the shower trees. They grow to eighty feet in height near water. They close in the late afternoon for the night (also on cloudy days). Drop in February and March when pods are conspicuous. Library downtown, Kapiolani Park, etc.

OCTOPUS or UMBRELLA TREE
(In Hawaii commonly called a Rubber Tree)

Brassaia actinophylla ENDLICHER syn. *Schefflera actinophylla*

This is a member of the Panax family from Australia. The blooms are peculiar with long spreading arms that suggest the octopus. First they are greenish-yellow, then light pink, then deep red. Then dark purple fruits follow (like little dried berries), these harden and the whole arm falls. Royal Hawaiian grounds.

ORCHID TREE
Bauhinia monandra KURZ

This small deciduous member of the Bauhinia family has pink orchid-like flowers along its branches. It is called a St. Thomas Tree. From tropical America, it blooms in spring and summer. Kalia Road Diamond Head of Halekulani.

PLUMERIA (Graveyard Flower) FRANGIPANI, RAINBOW PLUMERIA

Melia to the Hawaiians. There is a Gerrit Wilder variety which has orange-pink blossoms. These hybrids are a cross between the common varieties. The flowers appear on the bare branches first, then the leaves appear. They bloom most of the year. They are a member of Periwinkle family. The flowers have five oval-shaped petals. The stems exude milky juice which will stain clothing. Hotel grounds, etc.

PLUMERIA

The "pua melia" is the commonest lei flower. Its fragrant waxy flowers—white, yellow, pink and cerise—remain fresh for a long time. It is a native of Tropical America. In India and temple gardens of Ceylon, it is known as Frangipani. It was extensively planted in cemeteries in Hawaii at first. The natives wouldn't make leis of it because of this. Now, however, it is one of the most loved lei flowers to native and tourists alike. Somewhat like the Rhododendron in appearance, most shrubs lose their leaves. The Singapore Plumeria (*P. obtusa*) keeps its larger, darker green paddle-shaped leaves the year around. It is the lovely big white blossom with yellow center pictured.

DWARF POINCIANA,
Pride of Barbados

Poinciana pulcherrima LINNAEUS SYN.
Caesalpinia pulcherrima (L) SWARTZ

Ohai Alii to the Hawaiians is bright clusters of fiery red (also yellow) flowers which grow on the tips of this small tree. This is not a true Poinciana, but a close relative. It has five petals which are margined by yellow. There are long stamens and a pistil projecting from the center of each butterfly-like flower. It blooms most of the year. A member of the Legume family, it is the sacred flower of Siva in India. There is one on the University of Hawaii grounds.

50

ROYAL POINCIANA,
Flamboyant, Flame Tree

Delonix regia (Bojer) RAFINESQUE

The Hawaiians call this "Ohai 'ula."
This solid picture of color grows up to forty feet high in a graceful umbrella roof of red. Bare in winter, the flowering season is long. From early spring until late summer it blooms, with June usually finding it in its most gorgeous array. The individual flowers have five petals, one being white or yellow. Long curved (Continued on page 52)

ROYAL POINCIANA
(Continued)

brown pods hang on the tree for months
after the flowers and leaves have gone.
It is a member of the Legume family.
The leaves are fernlike, the flowers come
first—sometimes leaves and flowers to-
gether. It is a native of Madagascar.
French call it Flamboyant. There is an
avenue of Poincianas on Wilder Avenue.
(Scarlet or orange color.)

GOLDEN SHOWER TREE,
Indian Laburnum

Cassia fistula LINNAEUS

The shower trees belong to the Legume family. The Golden Shower has large clusters of bright yellow blossoms which tumble down making the tree look as if it was always in the sunshine. The leaves are large and compound leaflets two to six inches long. The flowers have five petals with a spike-like blossom. From the center of this flower projects long curving pistil and stamens. The pistil develops into the round black pod which grows up to three feet in length. This pod gives it the name of Pudding-pipe in India. A cathartic is made from its sticky brown pulp. The Indians also use the pulp added to their tobacco. They bloom from spring through summer with June and July showing them best. They line Pensacola Street between Lunalilo and Wilder. One on Punahou Campus.

KALAMONA, Scrambled Eggs
(Common Wild Shower)

Cassia glauca LAMARCK

This is a very commonly seen shrub or small tree. The clusters of bright yellow flowers look like scrambled eggs on the bushes on the hillsides. It grows wild especially in dry places. It has adopted Hawaii, but is a native of tropical Asia. The flowers and leaves are similar to its cousin, the Golden Shower. The foliage is compound, leaflets many and medium sized. It blooms most of the year. Hawaiian name has been transferred to this from native Cassia (*C. guadichaudii*). "Solomon in all his glory" is said of it. Solomon means Kalamona in Hawaiian. It is everblooming and has brown pods. Seen along the highways. Bark used medicinally by diabetes patients.

PINK AND WHITE SHOWER TREE

Cassia javanica LINNAEUS
(known formerly in Hawaii as *Cassia nodosa* HAMILTON)

Another of the Legume family from Java. Its branches are completely surrounded by masses of unevenly tinted pink blossoms. Each petal is pale pink or white with deeper pink veinings, giving a variegated effect. The flower has five petals with a tuft of stamens from the center. Blooms from about March through September. The tree is deciduous with the flowers preceeding the leaves. The trees are not too large, but are quite irregular in form. Kalanianaole Highway is lined with these trees. Also Piikoi near Wilder.

55

RAINBOW SHOWER TREE,

Cassia javanica + Cassia fistula (Cassia hybrida)

A visitor to Hawaii hears much of the "Shower Trees" that bloom here. One of the loveliest is the hybrid which is a cross between the Pink and White Shower and the Golden Shower. They bloom in all their bright array in a breathtaking great fluffy mass of color. No two seem to be alike unless grafted. They are from cream to lemon yellow to peach and apricot to rosy orange. They give a two-toned effect because the inside and outside of the petals differ. From tropical Asia, it blooms from June through August. Lunalilo Street between Pensacola and Kapiolani. Makiki above Nehoa. East Hind Drive in Aina Haina. Official tree of Honolulu.

SILK OAK, Silver Oak Tree

Grevillea robusta A. CUNN

Known as He-oka, Oka-Kilika, Ha'iku, Ke'oke'o to the Hawaiians. This big tree has dark yellow-brown blooms which jut out like fingers from its branches. Usually four fingers. Each individual bloom looks like big pins stuck in a pincushion. The leaves are fern-like with narrow pointed long dark leaflets like a palm. The tree grows quickly, sometimes up to one hundred feet. Wood is like oak in grain. It is one of the twelve best trees for reforesting in Hawaii. In December of 1938, 105,000 trees were planted in forest reserves. Blooms winter, spring, summer. From Australia. Lower slopes of Tantalus, behind Schofield, on Kauai.

PINK TECOMA TREE

Tabebuia pentaphylla HEMSLEY

Amapa-Hawaiian. Bright pinkish-lavender mass of blooms on big trees are another of the Bignonia family from tropical America. The flower is similar to the mainland petunia. It blooms in the spring. The leaves made up of five leaflets of irregular size from a common center. There are many small trees around Honolulu, but there are some large trees on the way to the Pali. One on Kimo Drive, one in Dowsett Highland.

58

TIGER'S CLAW, Indian Coral Tree—

Erythrina indica LAMARCK, syn.
Erythrina variegata var. *orientalis* (L) MERR.

Large, spreading, deciduous tree, bursting into pointed red pea-shaped blossoms in midwinter and early spring. Flowers are a deep, rich red on the bare tree. Long spikes jut out of woody stems on the ends of the branches. The individual flowers break out of the split side of a pointed calyx with one flower petal much larger than the others giving the effect of a pointed claw or feline toe nail. The seed pods too, resemble pointed claws. Native of tropical Asia, member of Legume family. Iolani Palace grounds and University of Hawaii campus.

WILI-WILI

Erythrina monosperma

Not illustrated.

There is a closely related Hawaiian tree to the Indian Tiger's Claw which grows in dry places on the Island. It has pale red, orange or yellowish flowers. The bright red seeds were made into leis by the Hawaiians. Now they use the seeds of the false Wili-Wili (*Adenanthera pavonina*). They have unusual, curling pods filled with bright red seeds. Grow in Thomas Square. The seeds fall in the spring. (See page 23, "Tropical Trees of Hawaii"— *Hargreaves*.)

HALA or SCREWPINE

Pandanus odoratissimus LINNAEUS

Screwpine family of Polynesia and Malaya, this produces the Lauhala so popular with the tourists visiting the Islands. The leaves are dried and woven into hats, mats, rugs, purses. etc. The tour drivers often "kid" the tourists telling them that the fibrous sections (drupes), which are a deep yellow when ripened, are pineapples growing in trees. Leis are made by cutting sections into short pieces and stringing. This is the female tree. Male tree is called "hinano." The flower is a drooping, whitish plume of hundreds of tiny, yellow staminate flowers loaded with pollen. The district, Kahala, means "Pandanus".

SUGAR CANE

Saccharum officinarum L.

Ko to the Hawaiians, this yields one of the most valuable products in the world. It is a perennial grass which probably originated in prehistoric times in Southeast Asia or the East Indies. It is a coarse six to fifteen foot juicy pulped stem. Grows in clumps or stools (largest known 360 stalks thirty feet high). Has saw tooth edges, blooms along about November with feathery, rosy-silver tassels that wave in the breeze. This is a beautiful sight, but the best harvesting time is just before the flowers appear. The plant is propagated from cuttings, not seed (five crops from one planting).

FLOWERING BANANA

Musaceae

(Chinese Banana called "Musa nana.")
Hawaiians call this Maia.

Each banana plant bears one bunch then dies and the new shoots (Keikis) around the base grow into another tree to replace the one that dies. An old Hawaiian proverb likens man to the banana. "Man is like a banana, the day it bears fruit"— that is, he dies after his work is done.

PASSION FLOWER
(Passifloraceae family)

P. edulis flavicarpa DEGENER

Passion Fruit Vine is from tropical America. It bears an edible fruit which is yellow when ripe. This is grown commercially in Hawaii for its fruit juice. It has a highly ornamental flower developing at the leaf axils. Calyx consists of tube bearing five sepals, five petals and a corona (crown) between base of tube and petals consists of a series of rings bearing thread-like fringe. Called "Liliko'i." Named for Lilikoi Gulch, East Maui, where seeds were first planted.

A companion book, "Tropical Trees of Hawaii"—*Hargreaves*, contains over 130 full color pictures of the trees of Hawaii with authentic descriptions and Hawaiian lore pertaining to the individual trees. Both Hawaii books may be obtained at retail counters everywhere in Hawaii, or they will be mailed postage prepaid anywhere in the world for $2.00 each in U.S. funds from the publishers.

RED TI   Pronounced "tea."

Cordyline terminalis (pictured) Tones of red from dark maroon to bright pink appearing in irregular strips along the line of the veins. They have cerise flowers and red berries.

GREEN TI

This grows wild in Hawaii. The blades are two to three feet long, very shiny, thick and strong in texture. They do not wilt easily and thus are used for many things. They are slit into hula skirts, arranged on tables for luaus, for flowers, lau-laus. They make a nice base for storing flowers. It grows on South Sea Islands, India and Southern China. It is a member of the lily family. Root stock used for Okolehao—a drink. One can place a section of the woody stem in water and have an attractive house plant.   ♂→

Publications by the same authors:

All books in this family are 64 pages each, all have over 100 full color pictures (some as many as 130) and all are the same size and format. Local names in local langu ges and text are different to reflect the countries and geographical areas they cover. Botanical names are included.

- "TROPICAL BLOSSOMS of the CARIBBEAN"
- "TROPICAL TREES found in the CARIBBEAN, South America, Central America, Mexico"
- "AFRICAN BLOSSOMS" (covers Tropical Africa, South Africa, Madagascar, Mauritius)
- "AFRICAN TREES" (covers same areas as "African Blossoms")
- "HAWAII BLOSSOMS"
- "TROPICAL TREES of HAWAII"
- "TROPICAL BLOSSOMS of the PACIFIC" (covers S.E. Asia, Malaysia, Ceylon and Pacific Ocean countries)
- "TROPICAL TREES of the PACIFIC" (covers same areas as "Tropical Blossoms of the Pacific")

All books can generally be found in book stores and tourist shops in the particular countries they cover. Or, books will be mailed postage paid via surface mail anywhere in the world for $2.00 each in U.S. funds from the publisher:

HARGREAVES COMPANY,
Box 895, Kailua, Hawaii, 96734, U.S.A.

IMPORTANT: If AIR MAIL delivery *outside* the U.S.A. or territories is desired, add $1.80 U.S. for one copy, plus 60¢ for each additional copy to cover extra airmail postage.

If AIR MAIL delivery *inside* the U.S. or territories is desired. add $1.00 for up to two copies, plus 50¢ for each additional two copies.

When ordering from outside the U.S.A. please send payment with order in U.S. currency, International Postal Money Order, Bank Draft, or check on any U.S. bank.

Lithographed in Japan